www.gardenpublishingco.com

Prophecy

The Garden Training Center, Inc.
An Apostolic School of Ministry

Copyright ©2020 by The Garden Training Center, Inc.
Published by Garden Publishing Company LLC
For more information, please visit gardenpublishingco.com

All rights reserved. No parts of this publication may be reproduced, stored in a retrieval system, or transmitted in any form or by any means, electronic, mechanical, photocopying, recording, or otherwise, without the prior written permission of the copyright owner.

This book is sold subject to the condition that it shall not, by way of trade or otherwise, be lent, resold, hired out, or otherwise circulated without the publisher's prior consent in any form of binding or cover other than that in which it is published and without a similar condition including this condition being imposed on the subsequent purchaser. Under no circumstances may any part of this book be photocopied for resale.

Scripture taken from the New King James Version of the Bible ©. Used by Permission, all rights reserved.

ISBN 978-1-7355464-1-4
Cover design by Garden Publishing Co./Whitney Whitt
Interior design by Garden Publishing Co.

Printed in the United States of America.

Acknowledgments

Holy Spirit is the inspiration for the content of this book, however someone put words to it. This book was written by Lauren Caldwell, Grant Hill and Kevin McSpadden.

This book is one of a series of books written and distributed by The Apostolic School of Ministry from The Garden Training Center, Inc. The series arises from the foundational teachings of the school of ministry, founded by Brandy Helton. Brandy wrote several sections that are included in each book such as "God's Love" and the prayers included at the end of each book.

Many thanks to the team of writers of the series for their collaboration to make the series available to the public. The writers are: Lauren Caldwell, Jessica Doggett, Danetta Ferguson, Elisa Griffith, Nancy Hadley, Robin Harmon, Brandy Helton, Grant Hill, and Kevin McSpadden. Each have sought Holy Spirit for the words He wants to speak through them. The result is a mixture of personalities and communication strategies that convey the total message in a beautiful, diverse way.

A special thanks goes to Nancy Hadley, and Chelsey Butcher with Garden Publishing Co., for their preparation and fine tuning of the text.

Encouragement and Prayer for the Reader

Beloved of God, these teachings are written to reveal Jesus Christ and His heart of love for all who call upon His name to save them.

God has sent His only begotten Son, Jesus Christ, to save all who would believe in Him and His Word.

God desires to reveal Himself and to give us His divine nature in Christ Jesus our Lord through the power of His Holy Spirit.

God is Jealous. He wants us to encounter His presence daily and walk with Him in glory – intimate communion - today, while it is called today, and forever.

It is my prayer that this teaching would so impact the readers that all would come to know and believe JESUS, the King of Kings and Lord of Lords, our Great God and Savior, and receive the PERFECT LOVE He has for us all as we grow up into Him and mature as true sons and daughters of God.

May you grow in faith and knowledge of your God and Savior and come to know the love that He has for you. I pray for you the Apostle Paul's prayer for spiritual growth:

Ephesians 3:14-21 The Living Bible (TLB)

"14-15 When I think of the wisdom and scope of his plan, I fall down on my knees and pray to the Father of all the great family of God—some of them already in heaven and some down here on earth— 16 that out of his glorious, unlimited resources he will give you the mighty inner strengthening of his Holy Spirit. 17 And I pray that Christ will be more and more at home in your hearts, living within you as you trust in him. May your roots go down deep into the soil of God's marvelous love; 18-19 and may you be able to feel and understand, as all God's children should, how long, how wide, how deep, and how high his love really is; and to experience this love for yourselves, though it is so great that you will never see the end of it or fully know or understand it. And so at last you will be filled up with God himself.

20 Now glory be to God, who by his mighty power at work within us is able to do far more than we would ever dare to ask or even dream of— infinitely beyond our highest prayers, desires, thoughts, or hopes. 21 May he be given glory forever and ever through endless ages because of his master plan of salvation for the Church through Jesus Christ."

In Christ our Lord,
Brandy Helton
A child of God

God's Love

God's love is good news! Don't believe the lie that God is distant, unapproachable, and angry!

God is love. He is the only true, eternal God. He is perfect and holy, and He is truth. God is One. He has revealed Himself in three distinct, individual, equal persons: God the Father, God the Son – Jesus, and God the Holy Spirit.

The Bible tells the story of God's perfect love. In that love, God created the first family to live on the earth with Him. Through their deep intimate relationship with the Father, Adam and Eve were meant to fulfill all that was in God's heart on Earth just like it is in Heaven, for God's glory and purposes. Adam and Eve were chosen to walk with God, clothed in His glory presence and were perfect, as He is perfect, and they lived in His beautiful garden, the secret place called Eden. He gave them His breath, life and power to have dominion over all He created and wanted them to reproduce that LIFE replenishing the earth with it, until all the earth is filled with His glory.

Genesis 1:26-28
"26 Then God said, 'Let Us make man in Our

image, according to Our likeness; let them have dominion over the fish of the sea, over the birds of the air, and over the cattle, over all the earth and over every creeping thing that creeps on the earth.' 27 So God created man in His own image; in the image of God He created him; male and female He created them. 28 Then God blessed them, and God said to them, 'Be fruitful and multiply; fill the earth and subdue it; have dominion over the fish of the sea, over the birds of the air, and over every living thing that moves on the earth.'"

God created His children in His likeness. He made them spirit beings, with a soul – mind, will and emotions – and placed them in a physical body. He gave His children the choice to love Him and to walk with Him in obedience to His every word. He gave the first family the power to overcome any temptation offered to them through God's adversary, the devil, who had rebelled against the Most High God in Heaven's glory and was cast down to the earth. The devil, Satan, brought great darkness and chaos prior to Adam and Eve's existence.

Adam and Eve were deceived into thinking that God was not perfect in love as Satan, the adversary, tempted them to believe that God would not keep His Word to them. Through their own will, Adam and Eve disobeyed the Father by eating from a tree that had the power to open their eyes to both good and evil. Through their choice of disobedience, they willfully gave their inheritance and authority over to the devil and his kingdom. Sin entered mankind, which produced death, eternal separation from a Holy God. Adam and Eve were banished from the dwelling and intimacy of perfection in the garden and were sent into the world as a fallen creation.

Father God knew He had to come Himself and save His family, and in His wisdom, He chose to send His Son, Jesus Christ into the world to save us and restore fallen mankind back to relationship with Him. Through His Son, He destroyed all the works of the devil and the curse of death. Hebrews 9:22 says, *"And according to the law almost all things are purified with blood, and without shedding of blood there is no remission."* Remission means to cancel the penalty, so according to the law there must be shedding of blood to cancel the penalty for sin. The Father cancelled the penalty for the sins of His children through the shedding of the blood of His innocent, holy Son Jesus, who was the Sent One, called and chosen to die for all, so all could live.

John 3:16-21
"16 For God so loved the world that He gave His only begotten Son, that whoever believes in Him should not perish but have everlasting life. 17 For God did not send His Son into the world to condemn the world, but that the world through Him might be saved. 18 'He who believes in Him is not condemned; but he who does not believe is condemned already, because he has not believed in the name of the only begotten Son of God. 19 And this is the condemnation, that the light has come into the world, and men loved darkness rather than light, because their deeds were evil. 20 For everyone practicing evil hates the light and does not come to the light, lest his deeds should be exposed. 21 But he who does the truth comes to the light, that his deeds may

be clearly seen, that they have been done in God.'"

Jesus was conceived by God's Holy Spirit in the womb of a young virgin named Mary. He appeared as the second Adam, in the flesh, with the choice to walk in perfect love and obedience, full of God's Spirit, as a man to do the will of His Father.

Jesus grew up as any male child did in the flesh but He had divine fellowship with His Father and Holy Spirit. At the appointed time, He was revealed as being sent from God to save. Jesus went around doing good and healed all who were oppressed by the devil spiritually and physically. He revealed His Father's heart and perfect love to all who believed through His teachings, grace and miraculous power.

Salvation means eternal life, healing, deliverance, protection, peace, wholeness, and forgiveness. Salvation came to all men through the cross, where the Son of God, the perfect One, was slaughtered as a lamb, bearing all sin for all times from a fallen people. Jesus bore the wrath of God against the darkness that separated God's family from Him. Jesus was punished for our sin and died to cleanse us from the guilt, shame and condemnation sin produces. Sin separates. Love restores.

Jesus was crucified, dead and buried, spending three days and nights in the depths of Hades, the realm of the dead fallen race. Jesus took back the keys of death and hell from that old serpent the devil, Satan, and therefore, all authority was restored back to Jesus.

Great Holy Spirit breathed LIFE into Jesus and raised Him from the dead. He appeared to His disciples, those who followed Him and obeyed His teachings. He showed them that He conquered sin, death and the grave and now, had the keys of hell and death, and would give ETERNAL LIFE to ALL who chose to believe in Him. King Jesus ascended back to the Father of glory where He ever lives to make intercession for us all, and He is coming again to the earth in power to establish His Father's Kingdom on Earth.

Jesus Christ is the head and Lord over His church, those who have made Him Lord and Savior, by believing He is the Son of the Living God and God in the flesh, who finished the work the Father gave Him to do. He not only died for our sins to save and heal us, He chose to give His authority to those He called and chose to follow Him as His disciples, His family.

Jesus has commissioned His followers to do the same works that He did while He lived on the earth.

John 14:12-14
"12 Most assuredly, I say to you, he who believes in Me, the works that I do he will do also; and greater works than these he will do, because I go to My Father. 13 And whatever you ask in My name, that I will do, that the Father may be glorified in the Son. 14 If you ask anything in My name, I will do it."

God loves us and desires that none should perish. He desires for His family to be with Him where He is. These books are written to inspire all who read them and to reveal the heart of God the Father, Jesus Christ the Son, and Holy Spirit in order that we might RECEIVE THE LOVE HE HAS FOR US and be CHANGED INTO HIS VERY LIKENESS. God desires to dwell with His family forever and ever just as He did in the beginning. How glorious it is to live in His presence and dominion, beholding His goodness, forever and ever, amen.

The book of Revelation describes the time that is coming when all things are made new according to God's heart of love:

Revelation 21:1-7
"1 Now I saw a new heaven and a new earth, for the first heaven and the first earth had passed away. Also, there was no more sea. 2 Then I, John, saw the holy city, New Jerusalem, coming down out of heaven from God, prepared as a bride adorned for her husband. 3 And I heard a loud voice from heaven saying, 'Behold, the tabernacle of God is with men, and He will dwell with them, and they shall be His people. God Himself will be with them and be their God. 4 And God will wipe away every tear from their eyes; there shall be no more death, nor sorrow, nor crying. There shall be no more pain, for the former things have passed away.' 5 Then He who sat on the throne said, 'Behold, I make all things new.' And He said to me, 'Write, for these words are true and faithful.' 6 And He said to me, 'It is done! I am the Alpha and the Omega, the Beginning and the End. I will give of the fountain of the water of life freely to him who thirsts. 7 He who overcomes shall inherit all things, and I will be his God and he shall be

My son.'"

To understand what is presented in the Bible, you must start by understanding God's love. The good news is that God loves you!

The Heart of It

Prophecy is a fundamental facet of the Bible. The Bible is the Word of God. A Christian's beliefs are based upon the faithful evidence that God's words have never failed or become untrue. There are many facets of prophecy, but basically, prophecy can be summed up in this statement:

Prophecy is speaking forth the thoughts, intentions, and plans of God Almighty's heart and will.

When you hear the word "prophecy," you may think of a man referred to as a prophet crying out, "Thus sayeth the Lord!" In simple terms, yes, prophesies of God are spoken by the prophets of God but when you read our definition again you see that prophecy includes not just the proclamations, but the thoughts, intentions, plans, and will of God.

In this book we will begin to explain:
- God's promise of prophecy.
- The various types of prophecy.
- Purposes within the church and world.
- What is a prophet?
- How a Christian can prophesy and edify the body of Christ.
- Prophecy made practical.

- How prophesies in the Bible have been fulfilled.

Prophecy

Prophecy is speaking forth the thoughts, intentions and plans of God Almighty's heart and will. To first understand prophecy, Christians must believe God wants to speak and reveal His desires and plans for them, both for the believer's life and for those around the believer. At first, it seems preposterous that the God of Heaven would want to reveal these things to us, but the Bible reveals otherwise.

Jeremiah 29:11-12
"11 For I know the thoughts I have for you, says the Lord, thoughts of peace and not of evil, to give you a future and a hope. 12 Then you will call upon Me, and I will listen to you, and you will seek Me and find Me, when you search for Me with all your heart."

I Corinthians 2:9-10
"9 But as it is written: 'Eye has not seen, nor ear heard, nor have entered into the heart of man the things that God has prepared for those who love Him.' 10 But God has revealed them to us by His Spirit."

We read that when you search for God with all

your heart, you will find Him. No ear has heard about the things God has prepared for those who love Him, yet the Holy Spirit will actually reveal those things to His children. If you are born again by the Holy Spirit into Christ Jesus, you can seek the God of Heaven and hear with your ears His intentions and plans on the earth. We even read in Deuteronomy the secret things of God, yet to be revealed, belong to a believer and their children forever!

Deuteronomy 29:29
"29 The secret things belong to the Lord our God, but those things which are revealed belong to us and to our children forever, that we may do all the works of the law."

When a believer receives these revelations of God's thoughts, intentions and plans, the purpose is for the believer to speak it forth. The Lord God releases these secret things to be spoken to people. When believers obey and speak forth, they are prophesying, bringing the heavenly thoughts, intentions and plans of God into motion on the earth. What is the purpose of this? To create a path, or spiritual highway, for God's Kingdom to be established on Earth. Remember how Jesus prayed:

Matthew 6:10
"10 Your Kingdom come. Your will be done on earth as it is in heaven."

Prophecy creates a spiritual highway to allow God's will to come forth in an individual, a family, a church, or a nation. His amazing secret, unseen, unheard of plans, thoughts and intentions are to be established on the earth for us all. Prophecy makes a way for His plans to be established.

God's Promise of Prophecy

As we can see, prophecy is a gift produced by having a personal, intimate relationship with the Holy Spirit. As the believer strengthens himself in the Word of God, and begins knowing the Voice of the Holy Spirit, the Lord reveals to him new prophesies for a hope and future to come forth.

> **Joel 2:28-29; Acts 2:17**
> *"28 And it shall come to pass afterward that I will pour out My Spirit on all flesh: your sons and your daughters shall prophecy, Your old men shall dream dreams, your young men shall see visions, 29 and also on My menservants and maidservants, I will pour out My Spirit in those days."*

In the above passage, we read it has always been in God's plan to pour out His Spirit on us, men and women, young and old, in order to know the secret things of God and to prophesy! Prophecy then, through Jesus, is for all believers in the baptism of the Holy Spirit.

> **Amos 3:7-8**
> *"7 Surely the Lord God does nothing, unless He reveals His secret to His servants the prophets. 8 A lion has roared! Who will not fear? The Lord God has spoken! Who can but prophesy?"*

This verse in Amos teaches us that God does nothing on the earth without first revealing it to His prophets in order to have them speak it forth.

God's words have never failed or been untrue. They do not become unfulfilled. When God prophesies through His prophets, it shall be done on God's authority. As a believer, you want to know the true prophesies of God to see His good and perfect will accomplished on the earth.

Remember the Holy Spirit is the One who will reveal the secret things of God. As believers grow in knowing the Voice of the Holy Spirit, they will grow in stewarding His words and prophesies. Yet due to the sinful nature of our flesh, sometimes, as young believers, we don't always discern accurately the Voice of the Holy Spirit. This is why it is important to understand and grow in each facet of prophesy that can be found in the Word of God.

Types of Prophecy

The types of prophecy listed here are arranged from least authoritative to most authoritative. Each way a believer delivers a prophetic word is still prophecy, as a believer is speaking the intentions, plans, and thoughts of God's heart and will. But the depths of accuracy and authority rises as the believer grows in authority, faith and wisdom in the Holy Spirit.

1. Impressions or Discernments – when a believer is interacting with an individual or another believer, he may get a word or an image about that person and ask if it pertains to the person in some way. This is usually a form of the Holy Spirit gifts called a "word of knowledge" or "word of wisdom." Holy Spirit uses these to encourage and exhort an individual or group.

1 Corinthians 12:7-8
"*7 But the manifestation of the Spirit is given to each one for the profit of all: 8 for to one is given the word of wisdom through the Spirit, to another the word of knowledge through the same Spirit...*"

2. Dream or Visions – when a believer gets a dream or vision about a specific situation, or upcoming future event, sometimes the dream is not explicitly clear. Believers must always test the spirit of a dream and discern if it is a warning or an encouragement from God.

Acts 2:17
"*17 And it shall come to pass in the last days, says God, That I will pour out of My Spirit on all flesh; Your sons and your daughters shall prophesy, Your young men shall see visions, Your old men shall dream dreams...*"

1 John 4:6-7
"*6 We are of God. He who knows God hears us; he who is not of God does not hear us. By this we know the spirit of truth and the spirit of error. 7 Beloved, let us love one another, for love is of God; and everyone who loves is born of God and knows God.*"

2 Corinthians 12:1-4
"*1 It is doubtless not profitable for me to boast. I will come to visions and revelations of the Lord: 2 I know a man in Christ who fourteen years ago—whether in the body I do not know, or whether out of the body I do not know, God knows—such a one was caught up to the third heaven. 3 And I know such a man—whether in*

the body or out of the body I do not know, God knows— 4 how he was caught up into Paradise and heard inexpressible words, which it is not lawful for a man to utter."

3. Consensus by Corporate Body of Believers – This type of prophecy occurs when several dreams, impressions, visions and words of knowledge come from different individuals within a corporate body or church. Together, as one, they go before the Lord and then speak forth the overall thoughts, intentions and plans of God to the body. Accuracy of this kind of prophecy is increased because many believers are testing the prophecies. An example is seen of the church in Acts 15:28, *"It seemed good to the Holy Spirit, and to us..."* and in the following verses where believers come together to know the thoughts of God.

Daniel 2:16-18
"16 So Daniel went in and asked the king to give him time, that he might tell the king the interpretation. 17 Then Daniel went to his house, and made the decision known to Hananiah, Mishael, and Azariah, his companions, 18 that they might seek mercies from the God of heaven concerning this secret, so that Daniel and his companions might not perish with the rest of the wise men of Babylon."

Acts 21:10-14
"10 And as we stayed many days, a certain prophet named Agabus came down from Judea. 11 When he had come to us, he took Paul's belt, bound his own hands and feet, and said, 'Thus says the Holy Spirit, "So shall the Jews at Jerusalem bind the man who owns this belt,

and deliver him into the hands of the Gentiles." 12 Now when we heard these things, both we and those from that place pleaded with him not to go up to Jerusalem. 13 Then Paul answered, "What do you mean by weeping and breaking my heart? For I am ready not only to be bound, but also to die at Jerusalem for the name of the Lord Jesus." 14 So when he would not be persuaded, we ceased, saying, "The will of the Lord be done.""

4. "Thus Sayeth the Lord" – This type of prophecy is the most familiar. It is when a prophet, or a Christian, is speaking in the first-person as God's voice. This type of prophecy is either 100 percent right or 100 percent wrong. It is very strong, like a lion has roared as we read in Amos. The Old Testament Books of the Prophets are written completely like this when the Holy Spirit came upon them and filled their mouths with His words. This type of prophecy can still happen today as we read about Agabus, a man who was accurate in his prophesies to the early church.

Acts 11:28
"*28 Then one of them, named Agabus, stood up and showed by the Spirit that there was going to be a great famine throughout all the world, which also happened in the days of Claudius Caesar.*"

Acts 21:10
"*10 And as we stayed many days, a certain prophet named Agabus came down from Judea.*"

Purposes within the church and the world

Prophecy then, is used in these varying facets for many purposes within the Church and the world.

- To edify, encourage, strengthen, and build up the body of Christ.
- To reveal God and His great love for people.
- To reveal Jesus Christ to our hearts for salvation.
- To reveal to people how God sees them and loves them. He knows their hearts and everything about them.
- To bring vision and purpose to people's lives; destinies are revealed.
- To direct a nation's course or change kings, and kingdoms.
- To convict, cause repentance and deliver from evil/sin.
- To warn of evil or judgments.

What is a prophet?

Prophets speak forth God's heart, passion, direction, and give spiritual vision, for His Kingdom purposes. To be a prophet means one is called and anointed by the Holy Spirit to give consistent warnings, wisdom, exhortation, and direction to the Body of Christ. Prophets labor in the body of Christ to equip and train the saints in hearing God. They help launch the believer into their God given purposes. Christians are led by the Holy Spirit to go where He tells us to go. Often in a church body, it is those who are prophets who hear what the Holy Spirit is saying to do corporately.

Many believers wonder, is prophecy only for

prophets? In the Bible, we find many believers of God who prophesied but were not recognized as prophets of God. God desires to pour out His Spirit upon all who belong to Him so all can prophesy. Some are called to be in the 'office', or consistent role and function of the prophet. All believers have the ability to prophesy in the Holy Spirit.

How a Christian Can Prophesy and Edify the Body of Christ

As we've covered, God earnestly desires to speak to His people. In fact, it's safe to say God is always speaking in a variety of ways. Nevertheless, one of His favorite ways to speak to His children is through a fellow believer. It is genuinely special when we can recognize the voice of our Father coming to us from a brother or sister in Christ.

In 1 Corinthians 14:1, the Holy Spirit inspired Paul to command believers that we should desire to prophesy. Later, in verses three and four, He explains why: "*3 But he who prophesies speaks edification and exhortation and comfort to men. 4 He who speaks in a tongue edifies himself, but he who prophesies edifies the church.*" Modern believers ought to desire this very powerful spiritual gift, but the purpose isn't so that we can do something neat. The ultimate purpose of prophesying is that we may speak edification, exhortation, and comfort to our fellow believers.

So what does that mean? Simply put, edification means building someone up. It is a way of strengthening or encouraging someone by releasing God's heart to them. Many times, a person who receives prophecy feels loved because God demonstrates His heart to them through what is spoken. It can be very encouraging for someone who doesn't know what you think, feel, or do to speak to you from God's heart, especially because that shows God sees and acknowledges you.

Exhortation has several meanings, which include strongly urging someone to do something, warning them, or giving them advice. Exhortation often comes with an impetus, a strong urge, to act upon what was prophesied. Holy Spirit supplies the power to carry out exhortation, so it's no surprise that this particular form of prophecy can feel very motivational. After all, why would Holy Spirit strongly urge someone to do something if He did not intend to supply what was needed to get it done? This kind of prophecy is similar to a coach encouraging a runner during a race. The coach may be giving very heated instructions, but the runner draws strength from the coach's enthusiasm and often performs better by obeying what the coach is shouting! It is important not to mistake exhortation for anger, especially when exhortation comes in the form of correction or warning. The Lord's exhortation, like all prophecy, comes from His love. It's one of the ways He urges us on to fulfill our destiny.

Comfort is pretty straightforward to understand. When a believer prophesies to someone, oftentimes that person receives a great deal of comfort from knowing that the Lord cares enough to speak into his or her life. Many people, believers and non-believers alike, feel relieved to know that God sees and cares about what happens to them. Sometimes, we just need to know we are on the right track, so the Holy Spirit moves someone to speak confirmation to us.

Regardless of which type of prophecy it is, it always reveals God's love for the person receiving the word. That's the true heartbeat of prophecy.

Another important function of prophecy is its powerful role in evangelism. Consider the example of the woman at the well in the fourth chapter of John. In this chapter, Jesus asks a Samaritan woman for a drink from a well. She is quite appalled, since Jews and Samaritans were bitter enemies, but Jesus persists. Starting in verse thirteen, the conversation opens the door for Jesus to prophesy:

John 4:13-19
"13 Jesus answered and said to her, 'Whoever drinks of this water will thirst again, 14 but whoever drinks of the water that I shall give him will never thirst. But the water that I shall give him will become in him a fountain of water springing up into everlasting life.' 15 The woman said to Him, 'Sir, give me this water, that I may not thirst, nor come here to draw.' 16 Jesus said to her, 'Go, call your husband, and come here.' 17 The woman answered and said, 'I have no husband.' Jesus said to her, 'You have well said, "I have no husband," 18 for you have had five husbands, and the one whom you now have is not your husband; in that you spoke truly.' 19 The woman said to Him, 'Sir, I perceive that You are a prophet.'"

Jesus does not merely have the desire to meet this woman's husband. He is speaking by the Holy Spirit, who has revealed the sin in which this woman lives. When Jesus gives the woman a prophetic word of knowledge about her five husbands, her eyes are opened to see Him as a prophet. That opening, which also serves to open the woman's heart, gives Jesus the opportunity He needs to reveal Himself as the Messiah. Strange as it may seem, this woman receives comfort and conviction from knowing God sees her situation, and when Jesus reveals Himself, she is more than ready to receive Him.

Prophecy often works this way in evangelism. God opens the door to someone's heart by revealing something to a believer who has no way of knowing whatever it is God revealed. It's not uncommon for someone to ask, "How did you know that?" The believer then has the opportunity to explain that this knowledge came from God, that He loves the person dearly, and that He would like nothing more than for the person to come home to Him through faith in Jesus.

To summarize, prophecy inside the body of Christ serves to build, strengthen, encourage, comfort, and correct God's people. Prophecy to those who don't yet believe is one of the ways Holy Spirit opens a person's eyes and heart to recognize God's love through Jesus. Either way, God uses prophecy to put His love on display.

So you're saying I can do this? The short answer: Absolutely! If you're a believer in Jesus Christ and He is Lord and Master of your life, and you've been baptized into His Holy Spirit, you can certainly prophesy. Paul makes this crystal clear in 1 Corinthians 14:31: *"31 For you can all prophesy one by one, that all may learn and all may be en-*

couraged." That means exactly what it says – every believer in Jesus has the ability to prophesy by the Holy Spirit.

Psalm 81:10 encourages us, *"10 Open your mouth wide and I will fill it."* In other words, God is looking for vessels who will make themselves available for Him to use. It's up to us to allow God to speak in and through us. After all, what good is a bottle that sits on the shelf and never gets put to use? We do not want to be that kind of vessel. A useful vessel is always being emptied, re-filled, and emptied again. That's what they are made for, and that's what makes them useful, just like us! Therefore, if you want to prophesy, you need to pray and tell God, "Lord, I am available and I'm listening. Speak to me and through me, however You will!"

One of the biggest fears many people have about prophecy is that they will not hear God speak. Jesus has quite a bit to say about that. In John 10:1-5, Jesus uses the illustration of sheep and the shepherd to illustrate that His people know His voice. John 10:4-5 says, *"4 And when he brings out his own sheep, he goes before them; and the sheep follow him, for they know his voice. 5 Yet they will by no means follow a stranger, but will flee from him, for they do not know the voice of strangers."* When we know Jesus, we are able to distinguish when He speaks and when either He is not speaking, or else someone or something other than Jesus is speaking.

Finally, Jesus promised that we would be given what we need to say when we need it. Matthew 10:18-20 says, *"18 You will be brought before gov-*

ernors and kings for My sake, as a testimony to them and to the Gentiles. 19 But when they deliver you up, do not worry about how or what you should speak. For it will be given to you in that hour what you should speak; 20 for it is not you who speak, but the Spirit of your Father who speaks in you."

In order to prophesy, the believer has to: **1.** Believe God's Word that clearly states all believers can prophesy, **2.** Make himself or herself available to God by listening for His voice and being willing to hear and speak, and **3.** Trusting that God will provide the words when and where they are needed.

Prophecy Made Practical

At this point, you may be thinking, "Well, prophecy sounds great, but how exactly do you do it?" That is an excellent question! While it is important not to turn prophecy into a formula or a set of steps, here are some very practical things you can do to ensure that you are hearing and releasing the Lord's heart to your fellow saints.

The first and most important thing to do is bind your own flesh and submit to the Holy Spirit. You can pray something similar to this: "Lord, in the name of Jesus, I bind my flesh and my own thoughts, and I forbid them to interfere in any way. Holy Spirit, I ask you to speak to me, and I choose to open my ears to hear and my heart to receive from You. Speak, Lord, for I am listening." At that point, do what you've said and listen for the Holy Spirit to speak. Now, it is a distinct possibility that you will hear God's audible voice, but that is not usually what will happen. Instead, you may receive a picture, an impression, a word or certain phrase, names, or even Bible verses. Each of these are special and important – honor whatever you receive and do not discount it!

Once you have received from the Lord, ask the Holy Spirit to help you interpret what you received. You may receive clarification or additional information. You may also hear to deliver what you received exactly as you received it. It may be necessary to ask the Holy Spirit how He wants you to deliver or release what you have received. You can pray something similar to this: "Holy Spirit, I thank you for speaking to me. I ask You to help me interpret what You have given me. Show me how to release what You have put in me in a way that will glorify Jesus and build my fellow believers, in Jesus' name." The key is to listen and obey from a heart of humility and love.

Some more keys to prophesying on a personal level are the following:

- Test the spirits! It is essential to be sure that you are speaking by the Holy Spirit. No follower of Jesus wants to be the mouthpiece of demons, but demons will often try to insert their words into the conversation. When you receive something, ask, "To the spirit who spoke (whatever you heard or saw), I command you to answer this question: Is Jesus Christ your Lord and Master and do you serve Him only? Answer me now in Jesus name." The Holy Spirit, and all those spirits under His direction, absolutely adore Jesus and will gladly answer "yes" to this question. Every spirit that remains silent or has a negative response is not from God. Ignore what it says and rebuke it in Jesus name!

- Test the word by considering whether or not it lines up with the Bible. It is true that words from God may not always be found word-for-word in the Scriptures, but they will never contradict what God has already given us in His written Word.

- Examine the word to see whether or not it comes from love. Does this word encourage or exhort or comfort? If not, it is probably best not to release it, at least until you have had time to bring it to a spiritual authority.

- As with anything in the Kingdom, submission to authority keeps you safe. If you are not sure about your word, or if you want to be certain what you're hearing is from God, tell someone in authority over you what you heard or saw. Many times, this person will confirm that you did in fact hear from God. They may also discern that the word was not from the Lord. Do not be offended! The authority who does not release you to prophesy a false word is protecting you from a serious mistake. Be thankful for that protection and continue listening for the Lord's voice, testing spirits, and making yourself available to prophesy.

One of the biggest fears people have concerning prophecy is that they will be in a situation where prophecy is requested, but they won't receive anything. If someone ever asks you to prophesy to them, but for whatever reason you are not hearing anything, do not panic. Remember, the Lord will fill your mouth when you open it. Simply start to pray for the person and bless them. Many times, the words of prophecy flow out of you when you submit to the Lord in faith, and sometimes that means you don't know what you'll say ahead of time.

Sometimes prophecy comes through dreams or visions. If you receive a dream or vision, realize that they are often symbolic, which means it could take you some time to understand it. Do not rush to release what you received. It may be that you received something the Lord is highlighting for intercession. The dream or vision may be just for you. As with any type of prophecy, you need to examine your own heart and test the spirits behind any dream or vision you receive. It is wise to write down your dream or vision and date it. Many people keep a journal for this purpose. This allows the Holy Spirit to reveal the dream or vision to you as He desires, and when it is written, it is made clear and easy to understand.

Music can be a form of prophecy. Sometimes, worship leaders receive prophecy in the form of songs or words during worship. Many times the instruments themselves "speak" by releasing sounds that communicate the Holy Spirit's heart or intent. You can both prophesy musically and understand prophecy through music by focusing on what Holy Spirit is doing. Ask Him to interpret for you, and agree with what He speaks.

Corporate prophecy is when someone prophesies to a congregation or group. The word released is meant for the entire body. If you believe you have received a word for a body or group, first write it down. That will help you in both understanding and delivering this kind of prophecy. Ask the Holy Spirit to show you whether this word is just for you or for the body at large. If you feel led by the Spirit to release the word corporately, approach the pastor or authority over the congregation. As mentioned before, submitting to authority in this way protects both you and the flock. You may be invited to release what you've heard. It is also possible however, that the word does not "flow" with what is going on at the time. It could even be that the authority receives a check about releasing the word, and you do not get permission. Do not be offended! You have done what you need to do by obeying the Holy Spirit. Many times, your response to authority reveals what is truly in your heart, so be sure that you are staying humble and remaining in love. Love does not focus on self, so if you find self in the picture, that's a pretty good indicator that your heart may not be entirely right. Whether you are allowed to release a corporate word or not, it is important that you do not withhold what you receive. Remember, you are a vessel and your desire should be for the Master to put you to good use.

As you can see, there are several ways and situations in which prophecy can occur, but the practice of prophecy is similar in each case. The focus should be on listening to what God is saying, testing it to be sure it is from Him, and then faithfully releasing what He has given.

How Prophecies in the Bible Have Been Fulfilled

The Bible accurately foretells specific events in detail many years, sometimes centuries, before they occur. Approximately 2,500 prophecies appear in the pages of the Bible, about 2,000 of which already have been fulfilled to the letter with no errors. God speaks to humanity challenging them to prophesy as accurately as He does in the following Scripture.

Isaiah 44:7

"7 And who can proclaim as I do? Then let him declare it and set it in order for Me, since I appointed the ancient people. And the things that are coming and shall come, let them show these to them."

Apart from the Creator of the universe, flawless, perfect prophecy cannot be done! By declaring things centuries before they occur God confirms the reliability of Scripture as well as the reality that He is the one true God. The odds for all biblical prophecies having been fulfilled by chance and without error is less than one in 10^{2000} (that is 1 with 2,000 zeros written after it).

In the New Covenant (New Testament) the earliest leaders in the church encourage people to pay attention to prophecy and gain courage and hope from them. Events that occur do not surprise God because He is in control.

2 Peter 3:2

"2 I want you to recall the words spoken in the past by the holy prophets and the command given by our Lord and Savior through your apostles."

Romans 15:4
"4 For whatever things were written before were written for our learning, that we through the patience and comfort of the Scriptures might have hope."

Fulfilled Prophecies of Jesus

Luke states his revelation that Jesus spoke to the prophets concerning Himself in the following verse:

Luke 24:27
"27 And beginning at Moses and all the Prophets, He expounded to them in all the Scriptures the things concerning Himself."

Jesus is the embodiment of the Word of God. What is written of Him is accurate and true. He still speaks today. Are you listening?

John 1:1-3
"1 In the beginning was the Word, and the Word was with God, and the Word was God. 2 He was in the beginning with God. 3 All things were made through Him, and without Him nothing was made that was made."

John 1:14-18
"14 And the Word became flesh and dwelt among us, and we beheld His glory, the glory as of the only begotten of the Father, full of grace and truth. 15 John bore witness of Him and cried out, saying, 'This was He of whom I said, "He who comes after me is preferred before me, for He was before me."' 16 And of

His fullness we have all received, and grace for grace. 17 For the law was given through Moses, but grace and truth came through Jesus Christ. 18 No one has seen God at any time. The only begotten Son, who is in the bosom of the Father, He has declared Him."

God appointed many prophets to be His spokesmen to His chosen people, Israel, throughout history such as Isaiah, Zechariah, Micah. The words of the prophets are recorded in the Old Testament. Much of what was prophesied was about Jesus, the coming Messiah. Jesus revealed Himself in person to the Apostles as well as to many others in His time, and those accounts are reported in the New Testament. So, what was prophesied in the Old Testament is fulfilled in the New Testament through Jesus. There are too many prophesies of Jesus to write out here in this booklet, but below is a selection of Old Testament prophecies Jesus fulfilled throughout His life. So, the prophecy from the Old Testament is followed by the record of the fulfillment in the New Testament. Through Holy Spirit, Jesus will reveal more of Himself to you as you explore the Scriptures. What Jesus reveals or says to you is His ongoing testimony.

Prophecies Concerning the Birth of Jesus

Genesis 3:15 declares that the Savior, Messiah, will be born of a woman which would make Him our human representative. Jesus would overcome the authority Satan had taken from humanity. He does this as both God and a member of mankind. Because He was human Jesus was susceptible to pain, suffering, and death which is represented by bruising His heel.

Genesis 3:15

"15 And I will put enmity between you and the woman, and between your seed (children) and her Seed (children); He shall bruise your head, and you shall bruise His heel."

The fulfillment of this prophecy that the Savior will be born of a woman thus becoming human is found in Galatians 4:4-5:

"4 But when the fullness of the time had come, God sent forth His Son, born of a woman, born under the law, 5 to redeem those who were under the law, that we might receive the adoption as sons."

Isaiah 7:14 declares that the Messiah will be born of a virgin:

"14 Therefore, the Lord Himself will give you a sign: Behold, the virgin shall conceive and bear a son, and you shall call his name Immanuel."

The fulfillment of this prophecy is found in Matthew 1:18:

"18 Now the birth of Jesus Christ was as follows: After His mother Mary was betrothed to Joseph, before they came together, she was found with child of the Holy Spirit."

In Psalm 2:7 David declares that the Messiah will be the Son (Jesus) of the Lord God:

"7 I will declare the decree: the Lord has said to Me, 'You are My Son, today I have begotten

You.'"

The fulfillment of this prophecy is found in Matthew 3:17:

"17 And suddenly a voice came from heaven, saying, 'This is my beloved Son, in whom I am well pleased.'"

In Genesis 22:18 God declares to Abraham that the Messiah will come from the seed (offspring) of Abraham:

"18 In your seed all the nations of the earth shall be blessed, because you have obeyed My voice."

The fulfillment of this prophecy is found in Matthew 1:1:

"1 This is the genealogy of Jesus the Messiah the son of David, the son of Abraham."

Isaiah 11:1 declares that the Messiah would come from the family line of Jesse. (A rod, stem, branch, and roots are analogies that represent family line.)

"1 There shall come forth a Rod from the stem of Jesse, and a Branch shall grow out of his roots."

The fulfillment of this prophecy is found in Luke 3:23, 32:

"23 Now Jesus himself began his ministry at about thirty years of age being (as was supposed) the son of Joseph, the son of Heli...32

the son of Jesse..."

Jeremiah 23:5 declares that the Messiah would come from the House of David: (A Branch of righteousness and a king related to the attributes and role of the Messiah.)

"5 'Behold, the days are coming,' says the Lord, 'that I will raise to David a Branch of righteousness; A king shall reign and prosper and execute judgment and righteousness in the earth."

The fulfillment of this prophecy is found in the same family line designation in Luke 3:23, 31, so God is being very specific about the genealogy.

"23 Now Jesus himself began his ministry at about thirty years of age being (as was supposed) the son of Joseph, the son of Heli...31 the son of Melea, the son of Menan, the son of Mattathah, the son of Nathan, the son of David."

In Micah 5:2 God declares through Micah the prophet that the Messiah would be born at Bethlehem: (Ephrathah means fruitful.)

"2 But you, Bethlehem Ephrathah, Though you are little among the thousands of Judah, yet out of you shall come forth to Me The One to be Ruler in Israel, whose goings forth are from of old, from everlasting."

The fulfillment of this prophecy is found in Matthew 2:1:

"1 Now after Jesus was born in Bethlehem of

Judea in the days of Herod the king, behold, wise men from the East came to Jerusalem."

Prophecies Concerning the Nature of Jesus

Hundreds of years before Jesus' birth the prophet Micah declares the Messiah's existence before time was created as well as His exact birth place:

Micah 5:2
"2 But you, Bethlehem Ephrathah, Though you are little among the thousands of Judah, Yet out of you shall come forth to Me The One to be Ruler in Israel, Whose goings forth are from of old, From everlasting."

God through Paul asserts that Jesus is the focus of this fulfilled prophecy in Colossians 1:17:

"17 And He is before all things, and in Him all things consist."

In Isaiah 7:14 the prophet Isaiah declares that the Messiah shall be Immanuel which means "God with us."

"14 Therefore, the Lord Himself will give you a sign: Behold, the virgin shall conceive and bear a Son, and shall call His name Immanuel."

The fulfillment of Isaiah's prophecy in Isaiah 7:14 is found in Matthew 1:23:

"23 'Behold, the virgin shall be with child, and bear a Son, and they shall call His name Immanuel,' which is translated, 'God with us.'"

In Deuteronomy 18:18 God through Moses declares that the Messiah shall be a prophet as Moses was to the Israelites:

"18 I will raise up for them a Prophet like you from among their brethren, and will put My words in His mouth, and He shall speak to them all that I command Him."

The fulfillment of this prophecy is found in Hebrew 3:1:

"1 Therefore, holy brethren, partakers of the heavenly calling, consider the Apostle and High Priest of our confession, Christ Jesus."

In Psalm 2:6 through the psalmist God declares that the Messiah shall be a king in the manner of David who ruled Israel from Mount Zion:

"6 Yet I have set My King on My holy hill of Zion."

The fulfillment of this prophecy is found in Matthew 27:37:

"37 And they put up over His head the accusation written against Him: THIS IS JESUS THE KING OF THE JEWS."

Isaiah 11:2 declares that the Messiah shall have the special anointing of the embodiment of the Spirit of God, His Holy Spirit:

"2 The Spirit of the Lord shall rest upon Him, the Spirit of wisdom and understanding, the Spirit of counsel and might, the Spirit of knowledge and of the fear of the Lord."

The fulfillment of this prophecy is found in Matthew 3:16-17:

"16 When He had been baptized, Jesus came up immediately from the water; and behold, the heavens were opened to Him, and He saw the Spirit of God descending like a dove and alighting upon Him. 17 And suddenly a voice came from heaven, saying, 'This is My beloved Son, in whom I am well pleased.'"

Psalm 69:9 declares the Messiah's zeal or holy passion for God. The psalmist describes the rejection or reproaches of those who are not as passionate as He is for God:

"9 Because zeal for Your house has eaten me up, And the reproaches of those who reproach You have fallen on me."

The fulfillment of this prophecy is found in John 2:15-16:

"15 When He (Jesus) had made a whip of cords, He drove them all out of the temple, with the sheep and the oxen, and poured out the changers' money and overturned the tables. 16 And He said to those who sold doves, 'Take these things away! Do not make My Father's house a house of merchandise!'"

Prophecies Concerning His Ministry

Isaiah 35:5-6 declares that the Messiah shall have a ministry of miracles to overcome all the perfection of creation which was lost in the fall of mankind in the Garden of Eden.

> "5 Then the eyes of the blind shall be opened, and the ears of the deaf shall be unstopped. 6 Then the lame shall leap like a deer, and the tongue of the dumb sing. For waters shall burst forth in the wilderness, and streams in the desert."

The fulfillment of this prophecy is found in Matthew 9:35:

> "35 Then Jesus went about all the cities and villages, teaching in their synagogues, preaching the gospel of the kingdom, and healing every sickness and every disease among the people."

Zechariah 9:9 declared that the Messiah was to enter Jerusalem on donkey. Cities or nations are often referred to as mothers and daughters, which represent all of the inhabitants of the land:

> "9 Rejoice greatly, O daughter of Zion! Shout, O daughter of Jerusalem! Behold, your King is coming to you; He is just and having salvation, lowly and riding on a donkey, a colt, the foal of a donkey."

The fulfillment of this prophecy is found in Luke 19:35-37:

> "35 Then they (the disciples) brought him (the donkey) to Jesus. And they threw their own clothes on the colt, and they set Jesus on him. 36 And as He went, many spread their clothes on the road. 37 Then, as He was now drawing near the descent of the Mount of Olives (outside

of Jerusalem), the whole multitude of the disciples began to rejoice and praise God with a loud voice for all the mighty works they had seen."

Prophecies Concerning Events after His Burial

In Psalm 16:10 David declares the Messiah's resurrection as he prophesies that the body of the Messiah will not remain in the Hebrew abode for the dead known as Sheol:

"10 For You will not leave my soul in Sheol, nor will You allow Your Holy One to see corruption."

The fulfillment of this prophecy is found in Acts 2:31:

"31 He (David), foreseeing this, spoke concerning the resurrection of the Christ, that His soul was not left in Hades, nor did His flesh see corruption."

Psalm 68:10 declares the Messiah's ascent and return to Heaven:

"10 You have ascended on high, You have led captivity captive; You have received gifts among men, even from the rebellious, that the Lord God might dwell there."

The fulfillment of this prophecy is found in Acts 1:9:

"9 Now when He had spoken these things, while they watched, He was taken up, and a cloud received Him out of their sight."

Zechariah 11:12 declares that the Messiah would be sold for 30 pieces of silver.

> *"12 Then I said to them, 'If it is agreeable to you, give me my wages; and if not, refrain.' So they weighed out for my wages thirty pieces of silver."*

Judas Iscariot betrays Christ for payment or wages. The fulfillment of this prophecy of Judas' betrayal is found in Matthew 26:15:

> *"15 'What are you willing to give me if I deliver Him to you?' And they counted out to him thirty pieces of silver."*

Given that the Bible proves so reliable a document, there is every reason to expect that the remaining 500 prophecies, as well as those slated for the "time of the end," also will be fulfilled to the last letter. It is wise not to ignore these prophesied coming events because you miss out on the immeasurable blessings offered to anyone and everyone who heeds prophecy.

Revelation 1:3
"3 Blessed is he who reads and those who hear the words of this prophecy, and keep those things which are written in it; for the time is near."

Conclusion

God loves to reveal Himself to His people. Prophecy is one of the essential ways that God shows His plans, intents, thoughts, and ultimately His love to those who have ears to hear and eyes to see. There are certainly different types and methods of prophecy, but each type still serves to encourage, edify, and exhort those to whom the prophecy comes. Simply put, God wants us to know what He is thinking, planning, and doing, both at an individual level and corporately. He has never stopped speaking, and He never will.

Furthermore, prophecy helps confirm the steadfastness of God's Word. With so many prophecies fulfilled right down to the most minute details, believers can take a great deal of encouragement and feel strengthened in their faith because God faithfully brings about those things He speaks forth. His Word never fails!

With that in mind, believers ought to feel honored that God has given us the opportunity to be vessels for His Word. We are commanded in 1 Corinthians 14:1-3 to desire the gift of prophecy: *"1 Pursue love, and desire spiritual gifts, but especially that you may prophesy. 2 For he who speaks in a tongue does not speak to men but to God, for no one understands him; however, in the spirit he speaks mysteries. 3 But he who prophesies speaks edification and exhortation and comfort to men."* God wants you personally to build His church and encourage His people. God yearns for you to draw people to Jesus by revealing Him through prophecy. God desires to grant you the privilege of releasing revelation of Who He really is. What an honor for those who say "yes!"

Whether or not God has called you to the office of prophet, you still have His invitation to prophesy by His magnificent Holy Spirit. Will you make yourself available to hear Him? Will you obey Him in releasing what He has said? Are you willing to be His vessel? If so, then you can eagerly expect Him to speak through you to a world that desperately needs to hear Him!

Prayer for Salvation

If you have not made Jesus Christ your personal Lord and Savior, and you desire this with all your heart, then please, join me in prayer:

"Heavenly Father, I choose to believe with all my heart, Your love for me. I believe that Jesus Christ is Your Son, the Son of God, and that He is God in the flesh. I believe that You sent Him to this earth to save me. Thank You. I believe He died on the cross for my sins and He was dead and buried three days, and then rose again from the dead and that He ascended to Heaven and is now seated at Your right hand and is returning again.

Father, please forgive me for all my sin and iniquity and I choose to forgive others who have sinned against me. I give You all my heart and choose to live with You forever. I believe I have been born again according to Your Word and that I have been transferred out of the kingdom of darkness and into the kingdom of light. I declare I am forgiven and healed! Now, I ask for Holy Spirit to fill me. Jesus, baptize me in Holy Spirit and fullness in order that I may know You intimately and serve You all my days.

Thank You, Lord, for loving me. Amen."

Scriptures:

John 14:6
"6 Jesus said to him, 'I am the way, the truth, and the life. No one comes to the Father except through Me.'"

Romans 10:8-13
"8 But what does it say? 'The word is near you, in your mouth and in your heart' (that is, the word of faith which we preach): 9 that if you confess with your mouth the Lord Jesus and believe in your heart that God has raised Him from the dead, you will be saved. 10 For with the heart one believes unto righteousness, and with the mouth confession is made unto salvation. 11 For the Scripture says, 'Whoever believes on Him will not be put to shame.' 12 For there is no distinction between Jew and Greek, for the same Lord over all is rich to all who call upon Him. 13 For 'whoever calls on the name of the Lord shall be saved.'"

John 3:3-8, 16-18
"3 Jesus answered and said to him, 'Most assuredly, I say to you, unless one is born again, he cannot see the kingdom of God.' 4 Nicodemus said to Him, 'How can a man be born when he is old? Can he enter a second time into his mother's womb and be born?' 5 Jesus answered, 'Most assuredly, I say to you, unless one is born of water and the Spirit, he cannot enter the kingdom of God. 6 That which is born of the flesh is flesh, and that which is born of the Spirit is spirit. 7 Do not marvel that I said

to you, "You must be born again." 8 The wind blows where it wishes, and you hear the sound of it, but cannot tell where it comes from and where it goes. So is everyone who is born of the Spirit.'"

"16 For God so loved the world that He gave His only begotten Son, that whoever believes in Him should not perish but have everlasting life. 17 For God did not send His Son into the world to condemn the world, but that the world through Him might be saved. 18 'He who believes in Him is not condemned; but he who does not believe is condemned already, because he has not believed in the name of the only begotten Son of God.'"

II Corinthians 5:17

"17 Therefore, if anyone is in Christ, he is a new creation; old things have passed away; behold, all things have become new."

I Corinthians 15:3-5

"3 For I delivered to you first of all that which I also received: that Christ died for our sins according to the Scriptures, 4 and that He was buried, and that He rose again the third day according to the Scriptures, 5 and that He was seen by Cephas, then by the twelve."

II Corinthians 5:21

"21 For He made Him who knew no sin to be sin for us, that we might become the righteousness of God in Him."

Colossians 1:13-14

"13 He has delivered us from the power of dark-

ness and conveyed us into the kingdom of the Son of His love, 14 in whom we have redemption through His blood, the forgiveness of sins."

Luke 11:9-13

"9 So I say to you, ask, and it will be given to you; seek, and you will find; knock, and it will be opened to you. 10 For everyone who asks receives, and he who seeks finds, and to him who knocks it will be opened. 11 If a son asks for bread from any father among you, will he give him a stone? Or if he asks for a fish, will he give him a serpent instead of a fish? 12 Or if he asks for an egg, will he offer him a scorpion? 13 If you then, being evil, know how to give good gifts to your children, how much more will your heavenly Father give the Holy Spirit to those who ask Him!"

Acts 1:8

"8 But you shall receive power when the Holy Spirit has come upon you; and you shall be witnesses to Me in Jerusalem, and in all Judea and Samaria, and to the end of the earth."

I Timothy 3:16

"16 And without controversy great is the mystery of godliness:

*God was manifested in the flesh,
Justified in the Spirit,
Seen by angels,
Preached among the Gentiles,
Believed on in the world,
Received up in glory."*

Fresh Infilling of Holy Spirit

Acts 1:8
"8 But you shall receive power when the Holy Spirit has come upon you; and you shall be witnesses to Me in Jerusalem, and in all Judea and Samaria, and to the end of the earth."

If you have been born again and filled with Holy Spirit and you desire MORE and want to encounter the Lord's presence afresh and anew, please join me in prayer:

"Father, in the name of Jesus, I thank You for loving me and I ask according to Ephesians 1:17-19, that You would give me the spirit of wisdom and revelation in the knowledge of Him, Jesus, and the eyes of my understanding would be enlightened; that I may know what is the hope of His calling and what are the riches of the glory of His inheritance in the saints, and what is the exceeding greatness of His power toward us who believe, according to the working of His mighty power towards us who believe, according to the working of His mighty power which He worked in Christ when He raised Him from the dead and seated Him at His right hand in the heavenly places. Amen.

Father, according to Colossians 3:9-12, I ask in Jesus name, that I would be filled with the knowledge of His will in all wisdom and spiritual understanding; that I would walk worthy of the Lord, fully pleasing Him, being fruitful in every good work and increasing in the knowledge of God; strengthened with all might, according to His glorious power. Amen.

I surrender and yield my life to the fullness of Holy Spirit; His power and anointing; the spirit of wisdom and revelation; counsel and might; the spirit of the fear of the Lord and knowledge according to Isaiah 11:2, in Jesus' name. Amen."

The Garden Training Center, Inc.
The Apostolic School of Ministry

The Garden Apostolic Training Center is a place that fosters spiritual growth. The center provides training to equip believers in Jesus Christ for the work of the ministry and to be victorious and free in all areas of their lives through the supernatural empowerment of the Holy Spirit. For more information check out **thegardenstc.org**.

The Garden Gathering Church

The purpose of The Garden Gathering Church is to encourage believers in Jesus Christ: to fully embrace the love of God; to walk in freedom; to carry His presence and glory; and to be equipped and trained for the work of the ministry through worship, teachings, and impartation.

> *"It's all about Love. When you see His eyes of Love for you, nothing else matters. That's it. That's all you need to know."*
> -Brandy Helton

www.ingramcontent.com/pod-product-compliance
Lightning Source LLC
Chambersburg PA
CBHW020548080526
44583CB00013B/1057